Crystal Healing

Shelley Kaehr, Ph.D.

ALSO BY SHELLEY KAEHR, PH.D.

Edgar Cayce's Egyptian Energy Healing
Edgar Cayce's Sacred Stones
Edgar Cayce's Guide to Gemstones, Minerals, Metals & More
Meet Your Karma: The Healing Power of Past Life Memories
Past Lives with Pets: Discover Your Timeless Connection to Your Beloved Companions
Pythagorean Healing
Binary Healing: Pythagorean Healing Level Two
Platonic Healing: Pythagorean Healing Level Three
Top Ten Healing Stones of All Time
Lemurian Seeds: Hope for Humanity
For a complete list of all of Dr. Shelley's books,
Visit her Amazon.com Author Page

ABOUT THE AUTHOR

Shelley Kaehr, Ph.D. is known as one of the world's leading authorities on energy healing and mind-body medicine and is widely known as a leading expert on the healing properties of gems and minerals. She also developed several energy healing modalities including Edgar Cayce's Egyptian Energy Healing, Holographic Mapping and the new Pythagorean Healing Method, among others.

Her work as a past life regressionist has been endorsed by Dr. Brian Weiss who calls her process, "An important contribution to the field of regression therapy."

Visit Shelley online:
www.pastlifelady.com
Join the Discussion on Shelley's social media:
Facebook Fan Pages: Past Life Lady, Shelley Kaehr
YouTube: Past Life Lady
Instagram: shelleykaehr
Twitter: @ShelleyKaehr

ISBN-13: 978-1979151528
ISBN-10: 1979151520

Disclaimer

This book is not intended as a substitute with a licensed medical or mental health professional. The reader should regularly consult a physician or mental health professional in matters relating to his/her health and particularly with respect to any symptoms that may require diagnosis or medical attention. This book provides content related to educational, medical and psychological topics. As such, use of this book implies your acceptance of this disclaimer.

Some names and identifying details have been changed to protect the privacy of individuals.

To My Readers:
Know that the universe is a wondrous place and energy medicine is an integral part of my life that I believe in with every fiber of my being. That said, while energy healing can bring real peace to body, mind and spirit, it cannot replace medical care or good old fashioned common sense. Should you require medical attention, please seek out a professional. My books are not designed to replace the medical or psychiatric communities, and while I do believe in what I teach, I make no claims about any specific results you may or may not receive from practicing these techniques. Each soul is a complex combustion of energy and information from past lives, paths we agreed to experience before we incarnated, lessons and learnings we hope to obtain, and so forth. What works for one won't work the same for another. I do hope that this material will help you in a way that will be most for your Highest Good and that whatever form that takes brings you greater peace in life.
Sending You Joy & Happiness on Your Path,
Dr. Shelley
www.pastlifelady.com

CONTENTS

1	Crystal Selection, Clearing & Purposing	1
2	Crystal Geography	11
3	Crystal Structure & Shape	17
4	Crystal Spirits	23
5	Crystal Metallics	29
6	Crystal Water	33
7	Crystal Elements	37
8	Crystal Grounding	39
9	Crystal Healing	43
10	Conclusion	48
	Bibliography	50

1
CRYSTAL SELECTION, CLEARING & PURPOSING

Crystals are special living beings put here by our Creator to assist mankind. They've been around a lot longer than you and I, and if we're lucky enough to find one we resonate with, there is much to learn from these wise record keepers of the ages.

When a Crystal crosses your path and you feel drawn to use it, that is a very special connection, a sacred contract, if you will, and you should treat it like any other relationship – with honor and respect.

So how do we know if we are supposed to work with a Crystal or not? One of the most common questions I'm asked about healing with stones is how to select them. The answer is easy – by honoring the *feeling* you get when you're around the stone. If it feels good, then go with it. That said, sadly, many of us are sorely out of touch with our own feelings, and even those who do honor their intuition often get out of sorts and out of alignment, so this isn't always as easy as it sounds.

Feeling is not seeing. You can *see* the most physically beautiful stone in the world, but it might not be the best one for you. In my healing classes, I walk around the room with a container of Crystals and have my students reach in and see what comes to them without looking at what they are selecting so they are not biased by appearances.

That's actually a good policy to follow when selecting friends or anything else you want in your life. We are trained to judge everything, including each other, by how we look, but *feeling* is more important. A good real world example of this is the show *The Voice*, because people are judged by how they sound rather than by how they look, which is really awesome.

Likewise, that's the best way to select a Crystal. Obviously we want jewelry to be attractive, but let's say there are two necklaces that are similar in style. Do your best to pick the one that *feels* best. Not always an easy task.

Sometimes it's hard to listen to the inner voice, tune into those feelings I mentioned. We are so bombarded by media these days, the quiet intuitive self has a difficult time getting through.

For that reason, you might want to use a tool to help you get in touch with your inner self, so let's take a look at one of my favorites.

Pendulum

A pendulum is a Crystal connected to a rope or chain. Use pendulums to make your feelings visual by holding the chain between your thumb and index finger, then ask your pendulum to give you a signal for YES. For me, yes is a clockwise motion. Then ask your pendulum to give you a signal for NO. For me, no is a counter clockwise motion. If what I do doesn't work for you, that's fine. Find what you like and do that. There's no right or wrong.. It's the results that count.

For example, you could use a large cross to represent Yes and No. If your pendulum moves back and forth from side to side, that may mean yes, while the no might cause your pendulum to move up and down. Follow what your subconscious mind wants, because that way, you will tune into what is best for you. Once yes and no are established, hold the pendulum over the Crystal and ask, "Is it for my highest good to work with this Crystal?"

Wait for the answer, and more importantly, *accept what you get.* We all want answers, but tend to ignore what we don't want to hear. Listen to the pendulum because it is a direct connection with your Higher Self, and when you tune in at that level, you'll never go wrong.

Rose Quartz Pendulum

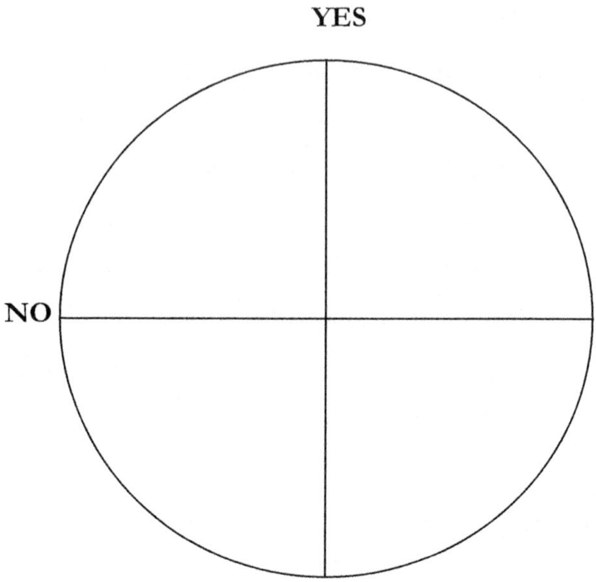

The chart above will help you program your pendulum to receive yes or no answers. Allow the stone to move along the access of the circle to determine whether or not the answer is YES or NO.

Muscle Testing with the Tea Pot Oracle

Another good way to get in touch with which Crystal to use, or find the answer to many of life's tough challenges is to do muscle testing, formally known as *Applied Kinesiology*. I do this all the time to gain clarity that only my Higher Self can provide.

While you don't need any particular tools to do this, years ago, a friend suggested I use a whistling teapot to help make decisions. You've probably seen the lightweight colored aluminum pots with the plastic handles and spouts, right?

To use this oracle, put the teapot on a flat surface, such as your kitchen counter, then extend your arm out straight while holding the handle of your teapot. The pot does not need to be filled with water. In fact, if it's empty, it brings a more meaningful result when you experience how heavy it is with a no answer.

One thing to remember if you do this is to state your query in the form of a statement, rather than saying, "Should I do this or that." For example, while your arm is stretched out, say the following: "It's okay for me to ask these questions." Then try and lift the pot. If your answer is yes, or affirmative, the pot will lift easily. This is a good question to start with.

Next, do a test question that gives a yes answer such as, "My name is John." (or whatever your name is) Then, do another test question. I typically say, "My name is John.". The pot will suddenly feel so heavy, you can't lift it an inch! It's incredible!

Next, make a statement about what you would like to know. You can say, "It is in my best interest to work with this Crystal." If your arm lifts easily, the answer is yes, if your arm won't lift, the answer is no. Trust the answer!

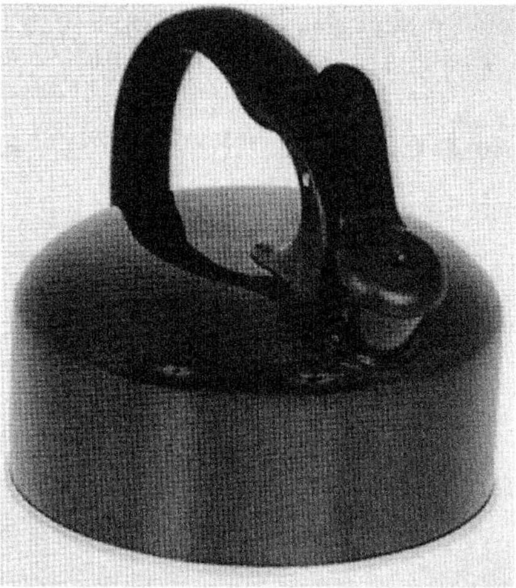

Use a teapot to help get in touch with your Higher Self.

Everyone needs a little help getting in touch with themselves from time to time. This is hands down the very best way to receive information that is for your highest good because the answer comes in the strength of your muscles rather than an outside source, which is why it's called *muscle testing*. When we do things for our highest good, our muscles are strong. If we do something detrimental, our muscles become weak.

You don't have to use a teapot either. If I'm not near the kitchen, I use whatever I can find. By judging things with my own inner strength, I have my answer.

Regardless of what tool you use, the point is to notice your muscles being either strong or weak, so you know, beyond a shadow of doubt, what the right answer is for you.

This technique works with anything. Is it in your best interest to take a trip or not, continue a relationship, apply for a certain job. Whatever. Try this. I think you'll feel more empowered following your own inner advice and counsel.

Cleaning & Caring for Crystals

Once you figure out which Crystal is best for you to use, be sure and cleanse your new stone.

All Crystal picks up energies from the immediate surroundings or prior owners, so once you select your Crystal, it's best to do a thorough clearing before working with it. By cleansing I'm not only talking about rinsing with water, but spiritual cleansing as well.

Here are a few of the best ways to clear Crystals:

1) **Grounding** – To me this is the very best way. Put the Crystal outside and allow vibrations to be transformed and within Mother Earth.

2) **Sunshine** – Clear Crystals love bright sunlight. Careful with colored stones like Amethyst that fade in the sun.

3) **Moonlight** – I love working with the moon. Lay your Crystals outside during a full moon. The stone gains extra energy from the lunar vibrations.

4) **Lightning or Rain** – Crystals thunder, lightning and rain. The electrical energy will charge your Crystal. Again, be careful with delicate minerals like Azurite or Kyanite.

5) **Sage & Incense** – Burn a sage wand or incense stick and allow the smoke to wash over your Crystal preparing it for the next use.

6) **Holy Water** – You can bless any water by simply willing it so, but there is something extra special about priest blessed water from a church. Sprinkle it over your Crystal, around your home or office or in the healing room for spiritual protection.

7) **Reiki** – Send Reiki or any other energy into the water, bathe your Crystal in that water, or send Reiki energy or the Reiki symbols directly to your Crystal to clear them.

8) **Salt** – Not all salt is the same. I recommend Sea Salts first, Sodium Chloride table salt second, and magnesium based Epsom Salts third. Crystals do well with it, but again, others may be damaged if they're too delicate, so use your best judgment.

9) **Power of Prayer** – Your simple prayer for healing instantly clears your Crystal. Envision the stone being cleared by your own thoughts, and then trust that it is done.

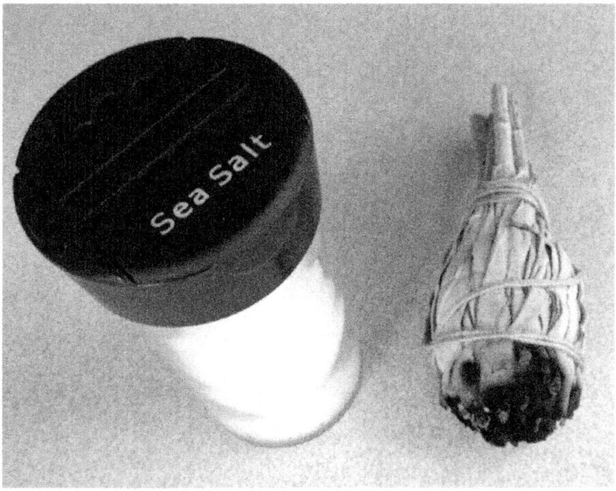

Sea salt and sage are awesome tools for clearing Crystals.

Programming

Once you select the right Crystal for you, the next step is programming. Crystals are natural transmitters and are quite empathic when it comes to the vibrational frequencies around them. What does this mean to you? You can tell a Crystal what to do – a process called *Programming* – and your new stone will serve you to the best of its ability.

That said, everyone has a special purpose in life, talents and gifts that they are better at than others, and Crystals are the same. Every Crystal has special abilities, and just like with people, for you to get the most out of working with the Crystal, it is best to understand what its strengths are from the get go.

Out of the spirit of respect and guidance "ask" your Crystal what it would like to do, or what it is best at doing.

Several factors will determine exactly how a Crystal may be of assistance.

Crystals are vulnerable to our influences, as mentioned before, which is one reason why it's important not to try and project your own agenda on to your new Crystal.

It's the same in a relationship. Let's say you're going out on a date and you really want a hamburger, but your date is a vegetarian. Do you push them into a thick beef patty with fries? You can, but you're not likely to ever go out with them again!

Crystals are the same. Sure, people can program Crystals to operate and function in any way needed. As long as the Crystal is "told" what to do, it will gladly comply. Crystals are givers and they will override their own highest purpose for you, so let's make our best effort to co-create with Crystals to get the best results.

What kinds of things can our Crystal help with? After determining their higher purpose, I've used Crystals to assist with making my computer work better. I've used others in grids by placing them in strategic locations outside and around my home for protection and healing.

The Crystal will show you its highest purpose. How can you get in touch with the spirit of your Crystal to gain its trust and understand why it has come into your life?

Try the following exercise to find answers.

Exercise

1) Sit in a comfortable chair.

2) Hold your Crystal in your receptive hand and close your eyes. By receptive, I mean your stronger hand, so use the hand that feels most comfortable to you.

3) Feel the energy. Imagine you can ask the Crystal to tell you what uses it has for you.

You might say: "Please tell me your purpose."

or "How can I best work with you?"

4) Once you ask the question either in your mind or aloud, wait for the response. You might have an inner vision, showing you what to do, or hear the inner voice, or you might just know.

5) Once you receive the answer, trust whatever comes to you. Allow yourself to believe you received the right answer.

6) Thank the Crystal for working with you.

7) Open your eyes come back into present moment awareness and begin the journey of working with your new Crystal.

How was that? Did you find answers? Good job! Most of all, it's important to trust your process and have fun on the way.

2
CRYSTAL GEOGRAPHY

The location where any stone or Crystal is found is energetically significant. Spiritually speaking, different parts of our planet have varying vibrational frequencies. Thoughts are things, so memories and events from long ago are imprinted holographically into stones.

Quartz Crystal is Silicon Dioxide, and yet, although the formula may be the same, trace minerals can cause the stones to look and behave differently in different parts of the world and play a role in how any stone will perform.

The vibrational frequency shifts around the planet cannot be understated. Haven't you been someplace you fell in love with the moment you arrived? Likewise, you've likely been to other locations you'd like to get away from sooner rather than later.

Different areas affect people differently, and the same goes for Crystals. I'm convinced this is caused by our past lives and the energetic blueprint we carry with our souls throughout the ages.

I may love a particular area and you may want to run kicking and screaming from the place. That's the way life is. Therefore the stones we connect to should resonate with us on a soul level, and connect us to our past lives in ways that nothing else can.

I believe we travel to re-experience ourselves from other lifetimes. Sometimes just being in a particular city can provide energetic healing by putting the missing piece back into the puzzle of our soul.

Crystals are of tremendous benefit to us because we might not have the luxury of physically traveling to different parts of the world, but we can connect with Crystals or stones from that area and receive profound healing – theoretically the same level of healing as actually going there.

How you react to Crystals can give you clues into your past. I've worked with clients who were literally repulsed by different stones, and I encouraged them to work with those anyway, and they wound up receiving deep healing.

Stones and Crystals shift our frequencies and bring much needed balance to our energy systems. When we are repelled by a stone, it can be profound to stay with it until the stone loosens up old, outdated and stuck energetic patterns in our energy systems.

Geographic Locations of Interest

Speaking of these differing energies, here are a few examples of some of the more popular and diverse Crystals from around the world t you may run across so you'll know what you're looking at:

Arkansas Quartz Crystal

The area around Hot Springs, Arkansas, is one of the best in the entire world for hunting Crystals. There is an extremely clean energy there that is hard to describe unless you've been there and experienced it for yourself. Hot Springs is one of my favorite places on Earth. I'm convinced that those who are attracted to the area are there for a reason.

The old historic downtown is filled with bathhouses with from the last century. People go there to drink and bathe in the healing waters, and there are fountains in the city center where you can fill your water bottles with the piping hot healing waters and take it home with you for free. I love it there, and I truly believe there's something to the healing potential in those waters which can likely be attributed to the large amount of Crystal in the area.

Just outside the city is Mount Ida, where you can go hunting and collecting your own special Quartz specimens. I've been digging Crystals there for years, and every time I go, I return home feeling refreshed and rejuvenated.

These days, many of the mining companies do most of the hard work for you by churning up the earth and redistributing it so you can easily get to the Crystals buried beneath the surface.

Mining still takes all day in many cases, but you're more likely to come home with some amazing specimens.

That said, even if you decide to forego the excavating altogether and find your Crystals in a retail store, if they're speaking to you and you feel drawn to them, that's just as valuable as if you found them yourself in the mine, so just go with it!

An old friend –
Arkansas Quartz I collected in
the Mount Ida area several years ago.

Tibetan Quartz

Tibetan Quartz carries the sacred OM vibration and helps dispel unwanted energy patterns that are detrimental to mind, body and spirit. Tibetan Quartz is becoming quite rare.

I've never been to Tibet, but I believe I lived there before, a phenomenon Carl Jung called *Anamnesis* – a soul knowing of one's prior incarnations. Most people drawn to Tibetan Quartz feel a special bond to Tibet, but even if you don't, there's still profound healing energy that comes from these Crystals because Tibetan Buddhist monks created a spiritual vortex with their chanting. Holograms of their sacred prayers are embedded within the Crystals and transmitted to the user. You can even hold Tibetan Quartz up to other stones to program them with the healing energies of this blessed land. I highly recommend you connect with this Crystal if you get a chance!

Tibetan Quartz is special because of the people in the area.

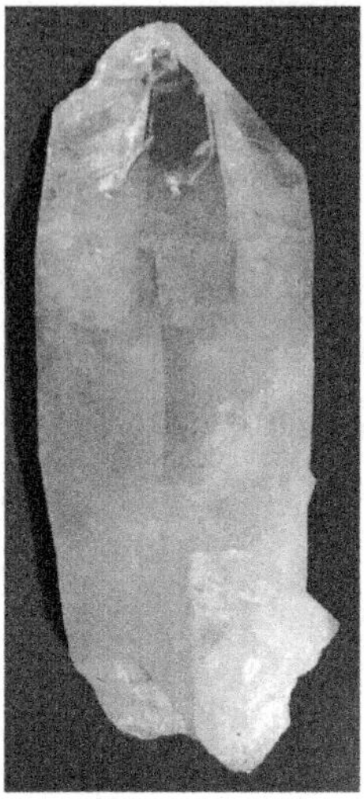

Brazilian Quartz

Brazil is the hot spot for Crystals and colored Quartz like Amethyst and Citrine.

Brazilian Crystals feel more commercialized than some of the others in this section, probably because it's such a big money maker for the region. The good news is mass production of stones has enabled more people around the world to work with them.

The photo above is one of my favorite large Brazilian Crystals. I did a major clearing on him (the energy seems male to me) to release energies from his prior owner by using the processes mentioned in the last section – placing him on the ground outside for a few days, cleansing him with sage and rinsing him with purified water. Once he was cleared, he worked wonders by helping me concentrate and complete important projects.

***

Regardless of which part of the world your Crystal comes from, explore and enjoy!

3
CRYSTAL STRUCTURE & SHAPE

In nature, Crystals have varying internal structures that coincide with geometric building blocks of our universe. Because of this, when we place a Crystal on the body, our cells begin to realign themselves with the blueprint of perfection that is inherent in the Crystal structure.

There are six basic Crystal systems. Knowing what they are will allow you to appreciate the complexity of Mother Nature in crafting these wonders of Sacred Geometry.

Because they are perfect, we can use Crystals to realign with our higher purpose and soul, and ascend regular consciousness to achieve our destinies and the reasons why we chose to incarnate into this particular lifetime.

Here are the six basic Crystal structures for your reference, along with examples and simple descriptions of their geometric shapes:

1) **Hexagonal** – Often found in column formations.
Examples = Quartz Crystal, Beryl, Calcite

2) **Triclinic** – Flat Crystals with sharp edges.
Examples = Turquoise, Feldspar

3) **Isometric/Cubic** – Crystals with many identical faces.
Examples = Lapis, Pyrite, Sodalite, Garnet

4) **Monoclinic** – Prisms, more rectangular in shape.
Examples = Selenite, Jade, Azurite

5) **Tetragonal** – Elongated and lean Crystals.
Examples = Rutile, Apophyllite, Zircon

6) **Orthorhombic** – Pyramids are a good example.
Examples = Topaz, Cat's Eye, Sulphur

For healing purposes, that information is not necessary, other than the fact it helps you realize minerals are all quite complex, and vastly different from one another. These differences can vastly affect your healing work. I believe geometric patterns are contained within our cell structure and we are compelled to use geometric patterns that we need more of in our live, or in other words, we work with the ones we are missing to heal ourselves, most of the time without even realizing what we're doing.

Here is a list of formations:

Quartz Crystal Formations

While Crystal Structure can apply to any stone or colored gem, Quartz Crystals have many specific forms that can be quite beneficial for different aspects of healing.

Formations include:

Phantom – Shadows of earlier formations are visible record keepers, storing information from long ago.

Fenster/Window – Framed window-shaped edges help you deal with specific issues by staying on task.

Faden Quartz – Flat pieces with thread-like centers can be placed on the body and align all energy centers.

Spirit/Cactus Quartz –Prickly with lots of tiny points help foster cooperation in groups.

Scepter Quartz – Wand-like structure moves and directs healing energy.

Gwindel – Stumpy shorter pieces with smaller points can be programmed for mundane uses such as helping your computer to go faster, or stronger cell phone reception. They are worker bees of the Crystal family and are fiercely loyal to the people they serve.

Sprouting – Smaller Crystals sprout from another main Crystal. Good for fertility and fostering creative ideas.

Artichoke – Crystals have tops that resemble the vegetable and make great pieces to place in a home or office to uplift the inhabitants with feelings of joy.

Platonic Solids

Carving Crystals into geometric patterns enhances healing power, particularly in the case of the three dimensional shapes known as Platonic Solids. In *Timaeus*, Plato claimed Platonic Solids are building blocks of the elements Air, Earth, Fire, Water and Spirit. Here they are for your reference:

Tetrahedron (Fire)– Four faced 3D pyramid.

Cube (Earth) – Six faced 3D cube.

Octahedron (Air) – Eight faced 3D object with two pyramids stacked on top of one another.

Dodecahedron (Spirit) – Twelve faced 3D object.

Icosahedron (Water)– Twenty faced 3D object.

Platonic Solids are revolutionary to use in healing. Sacred Geometrical shapes are universal building blocks, and by default, our physical bodies. When we place a Crystal Platonic Solid on the body, our cells realign in a state of perfection. Years my students and I built copper replicas of the solids. I was particularly fond of the Dodecahedron and sat in my copper Dodec every day while meditating. Did it help? All I can say is it felt awesome!

These days, I am enchanted by my giant palm sized Icosahedron.

Vogel Crystal

Another man-made sacred cut was crafted by the late, great, Marcel Vogel, a former IBM scientist who assisted mankind by developing advanced healing Crystals using complex sacred geometrical principals.

Crystal Wands

Crafting wands out of Crystal, even if they aren't the pristine Vogel cut stones on the opposite page, can be quite powerful for healing. Wands assist you in directing energy to precise points on the body such as the Chakras. As always, the Crystal you use will make all the difference in the result.

This beautiful wand has a Lemurian Seed Crystal point.

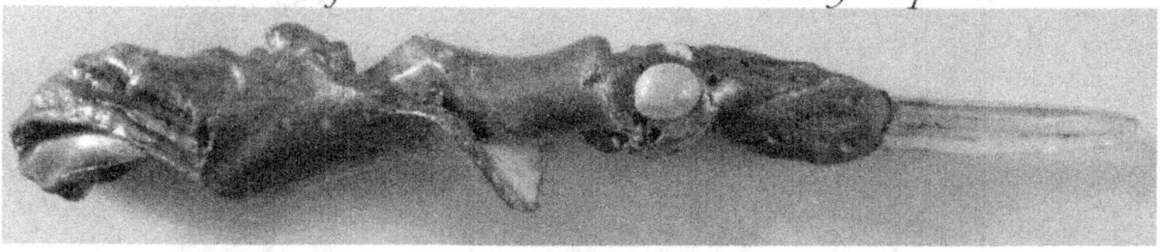

Crystal Egg

Like the womb of creation, Crystal Eggs are wonderful tools for healing. They assist with fertility both physically as well as the birth of ideas, concepts or new ways of being in the world.

To use these specially shaped Crystals, lay them on the torso during a healing, or in the case of a wand, run the Crystal over the body, stirring up the energy centers.

Stunning Crystal Egg

4
CRYSTAL SPIRITS

All Crystals have unseen spirit helpers, fairy folk, sprites and energies that work through and within them.

Nature spirits assist humanity with all sorts of things from world peace to simple physical healing. This is one reason why it's so important to ask the stone or Crystal what its purpose is for you so the being residing within can work with you for your highest good. While we are able to direct our Crystals, at times, Crystals can also be programmed in advance before we receive them by beings who wish to leave their energetic message or blueprint within for the benefit of mankind. Here are a few examples:

Crystal Skulls

We spoke about Crystal structure and the power of different shapes in the last chapter. But what if the Crystal was shaped by man for a particular affect, and therefore attracted spirits to it? That's exactly what happens with the modern day replicas of

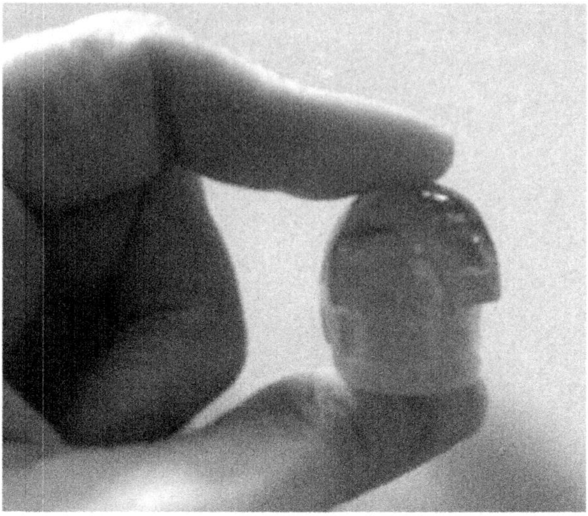

A tiny Crystal skull.

the ancient Crystal Skulls.

You may have heard about Crystal Skulls on TV or through *Indiana Jones* and other movies over the years. Archeologists discovered and tested thirteen Crystal Skulls that were supposedly proven to be ancient artifacts, yet nobody knows for sure where they came from or who made them. Did Extraterrestrials leave them here? If so, why? That's anybody's guess. Indigenous people claim the Skulls have magical properties. In modern times, Crystal Skull carvings are mass produced and sold by the thousands. After trying several, I believe there is indeed an ancient holographic energy within the skull structure itself. The smaller man made versions serve as a grid for the planet. The thirteen form a powerful protective circle of light.

I've seen some of the original Crystal Skulls over the years

– one in the British Museum, and another called Max on tour in Texas. While these originals are powerful beings, we don't always have access to work with them, so the mass produced skulls act as an antennae to connect us with the consciousness of the greater grid, keeping that protective light in place for the benefit of all. If you happen upon one of these little skulls and you feel drawn to it, try it! There's always a higher purpose.

Gaia Crystal

Gaia Crystals are inhabited by special beings who have deep connections to Mother Earth and our ancient history. Their purpose is to remind everyone to care for our planet and hold a holographic memory of the basic Crystalline structures throughout Earth so they are never forgotten or destroyed by future generations. All Crystals and stones are Gaia connected, but these are super charged with the energy of the Mother of All That Is.

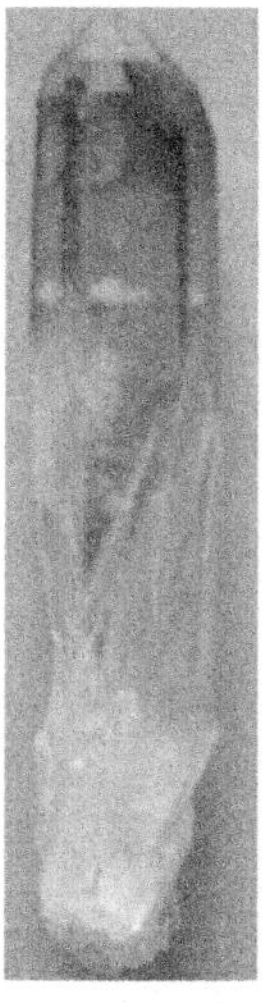

Gaia Quartz

Lemurian Seed Crystals

I have a special affinity to the special Crystals with ties to the lost continent of Lemuria. Lemurian Seed Crystals were once thought to be merely a regional Brazilian stone, but have now been found in several parts of the world.

Before Atlantis, the Lemurians were a benevolent race who implanted messages of hope and healing into Crystals. These ancient beings programmed specific messages holographically into tiny seed Crystals that grew over time, and those lovely messages can only be awakened by the right person at the right time working with that specific stone. The awakening is an energetic release that sends healing vibrations to the planet, and when enough people work with these Crystals, they cause a shift in consciousness.

Like the Crystal Skulls, there seems to be some sort of extraterrestrial gridding going on with the Seed Crystals. They are planted throughout the world in a very specific way to affect the frequencies around Earth and to benefit mankind.

Unlike many stones you will find throughout your lifetime, the Seed Crystals tend to find you, rather than the other way around. They will simply come into your awareness and, if you're like me, you will be immediately drawn to work with them.

Because they are already programmed, you won't need to take that step to work with a Lemurian Seed. All you do is simply hold the Crystal in your hands and allow the flow of love and inspiration to come to you. I believe these Crystals are helping make a positive change on Earth at this time.

Lemurian Seed Crystal

You can tell it's a Lemurian Seed by the striations in the stone which are similar to rings in a tree trunk. Each line represents embedded memory.

Spirit Quartz

Spirit Quartz Crystals, also referred to as Cactus Quartz, have a slightly pale purple color like Amethyst. They have tiny sharp points that form in protruding clusters which are said to contain the energies of supportive beings who wish to engender feelings of helpfulness and cooperation to our planet.

All cluster quartz helps group dynamics, enabling individuals to think of the higher good, rather than individual needs. Spirit Quartz has a super sweet energy. To work with them, leave them in the conference room, or any area where people gather with the intention of helping everyone come to agreement that is for the highest and best for all concerned.

Spirit Quartz helps people get along.

I hope you've enjoyed exploring a few of the Crystal Spirits. There are plenty out there, in all stones and gems, so happy hunting!

5
CRYSTAL METALLICS

Metals make a huge impact on Crystals because of the amplification factor. When metal is fused with Crystal, either in by nature or in a manmade fashion, Crystal frequencies are increased dramatically. Here are a few of the more potent kinds:

Titanium

Any Crystal covered in the metallic Titanium will send out a positive vibe that amps up your energy and imagination.

Rutilated Quartz

We mentioned earlier that Rutile is an example of a Tetragonal Crystalline structure.

When we talk about Rutilated Quartz, we are speaking of the tiny wisps of hair like metallic material inside the Quartz, the Rutile, which is actually made from Titanium (Titanium Dioxide, to be exact) a supercharged amplifier of energy.

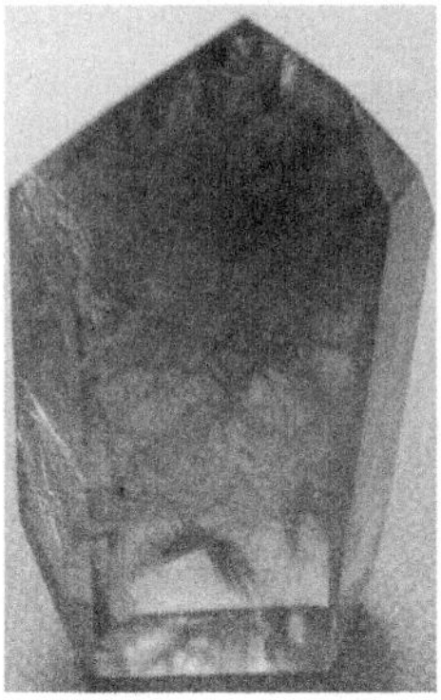

These tiny wisps of metal in Rutilated Quartz are Titanium.

Titanium Plated Quartz

Titanium Plated Crystals are awesome manmade coated Crystals that are wonderfully energetic, and help increase your enthusiasm and zest for life. Place them in your home or office for the best results and notice your happiness and wellbeing expand.

Wonderful Titanium Quartz Crystal

Gold

Gold is an energizing masculine energy. It is associated with the sun and the active, external principal for going out into the world and getting what you want.

Aqua Aura

When merged with Crystal, Gold can be quite astounding. That's exactly what you'll find in the phenomenal Aqua Aura, which is basically gold fused onto Crystal. You can get pointed specimens, similar to the Titanium example on the previous page, or you can find Aqua Aura in tumbled pieces, which are my personal favorite. Carry them in your pocket to increase prosperity.

Silver & Platinum

Silver is the lunar receptive and Platinum is the rarest of metals. Combine these two and you will have ***Angel Aura*** which is a manmade creation that causes Crystal to have an angelic otherworldly quality that connects you to higher dimensions.

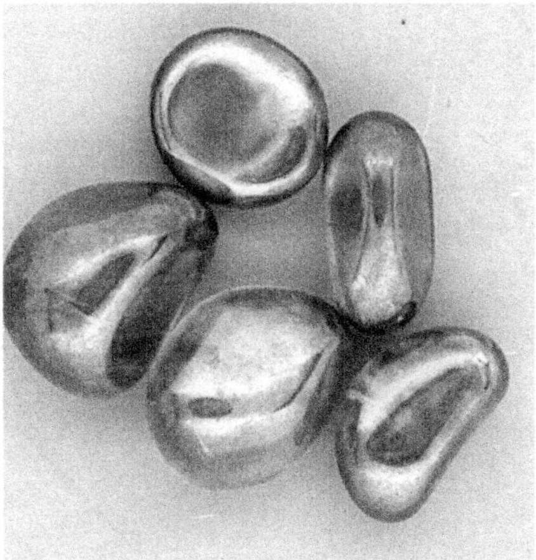

Amazing tumbled Aqua Aura is a personal favorite.

6
CRYSTAL WATER

Crystals can be used to make elixirs. The process is similar to placing a teabag in a jar to make brewed iced tea.

It is extremely important to only use a plain clear Crystal for this purpose, and not another softer stone, because it can leach off into the water and be toxic.

Quartz Crystal is tough and makes an awesome elixir, partly because of everything we've discussed already – Crystals are perfect formations within nature, and by aligning ourselves with that perfection, we reshape our cells.

When you soak a Crystal into water, you basically tap into the blueprint of perfection within the Crystal and absorb that into the water and ultimately into your body.

This next section will reveal exactly how to do this yourself by going through some simple step-by-step instructional photos on the process.

Enjoy!

1) Take a clear Crystal and rinse it off with water. Get a sun tea jar and place the Crystal inside.

2) If possible, use filtered water. If not, bless the water or send energy to it using methods described in Chapter One.

3) Fill the jar with water. Here you see I am using a filter that attaches directly to the tap.

4) Once you've placed your Crystal in the filtered water, take it outside in the sun and leave it for a minimum of twenty minutes or maximum overnight. Remove the Crystal and enjoy!

You can also make full moon water which tastes great too. To do so, follow the same steps, and then leave the Crystal overnight during a full moon.

You may notice that sun and moon water taste completely different, which is really interesting. You can truly sense the difference in vibrational frequencies when you see how different they taste than the purified water you started with. Amazing!

Birdseye view of the Crystal in the jar.

Again, the Crystal Water is taking the highest aspect of the Crystal and soaking it into the water for your benefit.

Please remember that if you do this, only use the clear Crystal. It's the best!

7
CRYSTAL ELEMENTS

There are other kinds of Crystal I wanted to discuss briefly. Some Crystal has chemical elements blown into it, and these can be quite powerful, depending on the element. Here are a couple of my favorite examples of this phenomenon.

Chlorite in Quartz

I am constantly impressed with Chlorite in Quartz. The unbelievable healing powers of the Bloodstone come from green Chlorite. When Chlorite is added to Crystal, it's a powerful healer. Some clients report the green will eventually disappear and be absorbed by the body and the Crystal will turn clear.

With the solid Bloodstone, the red specs disappear all the time. Red is colored from the iron hematite contained within it, but I've also seen clients literally suck the green color from the solid stones as well. Amazing!

Chlorite in Quartz.

Lithium Quartz

I love to discuss Lepidolite and Lithium Quartz as healings stones because they are so helpful to those with depressive disorders due to the Lithium.

Also these are amazing dream stones. They will put you to sleep and you will have amazingly vivid and often transformational dreams. The powers of Lithium are amplified by the Crystal.

The photo below shows Lepidolite in Mica. Lepidolite is a mineral form of Lithium. When the element Lithium occurs in Quartz Crystal, it looks similar to the Chlorite Quartz above, only there is a purplish wisp of material within the stone.

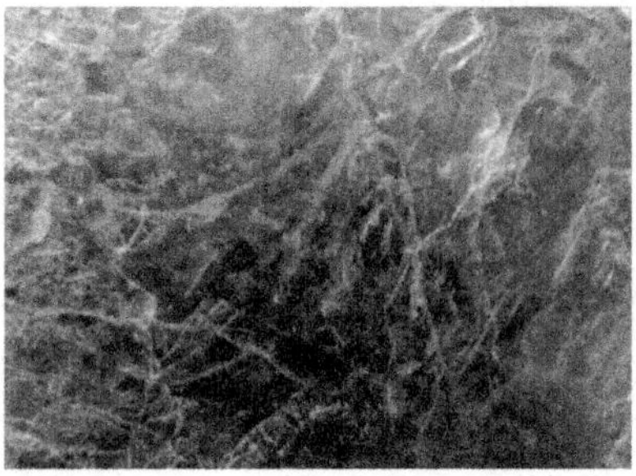

8
CRYSTAL GROUNDING

As a general rule, Crystal or any clear stones amplify energy and get things moving, while solid stones are more grounding and can often assist with sleeping, dreaming, and meditative states. Solid Crystal is no different. The pretty milky white Crystal has a special energy of grounding and healing.

Milky Quartz is really common around the planet. I often find pieces while I'm on trips and bring them home. On that note, whenever you are out and about, thinking of collecting rocks, seashells, or other natural items, be sure and ask if it is okay for you to take it with you, or if you can simply hold it, allow the vibrations to affect you, and then put it back where you found it.

I do this a lot. Recently on a trip I picked up a stone, wandered around the little village for the whole day, and then placed the stone where I was guided to before heading out.

On my last trip, I was walking around when my head jerked toward the ground, and there was a pretty white milky

Quartz. I knew that my guides or the stone spirits mentioned earlier in the book were speaking to me through the stone, telling me to pick it up.

Once I did, I asked, "Do you want to come with me?" I waited until the answer popped into my mind, and it was a definite YES, so I brought it home, and made it part of the family.

I have always treated my stones as pets, and I want them to be happy. After collecting about twenty stones and shells on my trip, I brought them home and asked exactly where they wanted to be placed. Some wanted to go out into the yard where I have quite a collection in my personal rock garden. Others came inside with me. As long as you do your best to honor what you believe the stone is telling you, you can't go wrong.

My precious Milky Quartz wanted to come home with me.

This Crystal sphere found me on a trip to China and wanted to come home.

Crystal spheres can be used for divination purposes, particularly when they are clear. At times, you can actually see images within the stone. Typically I am not attracted to solid white Crystal spheres, except when I went to China recently, and a white Crystal ball jumped out at me.

This stone is wonderful in the heart or center of the home to amplify energy and keep things moving.

As with most of my stones, this ball spoke to me on some unseen level, and I had to have it. If you find yourself drawn to any stone in that way, listen! It will always be for your highest and best. Who knows what you may experience through the spirits who assist you through your Crystal.

Another beauty I happened to stumble upon was the

stunning Snowflake Quartz specimen. Delicate like a melting snowball, this is a truly unique form for Crystal.

This piece is quite large, but I was guided to place it on my torso and use it for personal healing. I feel it is connected to higher ascended beings and illuminated information for the wellbeing of mankind. Consciously I did not receive any messages in particular other than the heightened sense of wellbeing after working with it. Now it sits in a prominent place in my office where the energy can benefit me as I work with my clients doing readings and hypnosis. The Crystal acts as a conduit to promote the proper energy to allow people to heal from past trauma and be open and embracing of future change. I mentioned the Spirit Quartz earlier in the book. This formation is similar, although it lacks the purple tint and brings through the white light of Source energy. It's a real beauty!

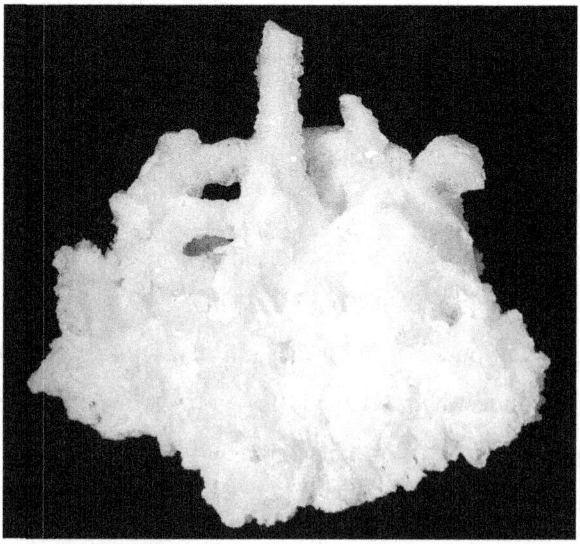

Stunning Snowflake Quartz brings calm energy.

9
CRYSTAL HEALING

So now that you know about Crystals and how to identify them, this section will briefly describe how to use your Crystals in healing for yourself and others.

Whether you are a seasoned energy practitioner or someone who wants to use the Crystals for your own purposes only, you can make wonderful shifts by following a few easy steps.

First we will discuss how to do a healing on yourself, and then we will expand that to include assisting others.

Let's get started!

Healing Self

When you are using Crystals to heal yourself, I typically recommend lying down in a comfortable place such as your bed. You can even plan to take a little power nap while the stones are doing their work.

So first, collect the Crystals you want to use. If they have not been cleansed in awhile, you may want to do so by placing them out on the ground, rinsing them with water, or sending Reiki as described in Chapter One.

Lie down and place the Crystals on your body. I usually begin with my torso, heart area, neck (the place just above your collarbone is good), forehead, and head. Of course you can't actually put a stone on top of your head, because it would roll off, so just lay it on the pillow, and let it touch the top of the head.

You may also wish to place a Crystal between the knees or lay a couple of pieces on your legs.

Remember, there is no right or wrong in this. I can describe what to do, but the bottom line is you are going to rest and lay the stones where you feel they should go, and know it's perfect.

Once you do that, lay still to the best of your ability. When I first experienced Crystal healing, I did not feel a thing for several minutes, so know if you can't feel anything, that's okay. It does not mean it isn't working. Just trust the process and know it is doing what it needs to do.

Go ahead and relax. Close your eyes, take a little nap if you'd like and kind of forget about it.

When it is finished, amazingly, you will open your eyes, remove the Crystals and you will likely feel more energized than before.

Of course you could say that's because you just napped, but believe me, there's more to it than that!

This works!

Healing Others

If you choose to assist others, you will add a few steps. When I work with clients, I typically have them on a massage table, face up for a half hour, and face down for a half hour, assuming they are having a one hour healing.

Your session may only take a few minutes. That's fine. I typically have the person face up, and then I place a Crystal on the stomach area in the mid section because the energy will vibrate to all surrounding areas of the body.

Then I put another on the neck, and do a sort of grid by placing pieces around the legs for circulation, and another at the top of the head.

Sometimes I place a Crystal on the Third Eye area or forehead, sometimes I don't. Often when I do, it falls off right away. When that happens, I assume the Third Eye is opened up enough and I allow the Crystal to fall and place it elsewhere.

If the person is laying face down on the table, I put Crystals all over the back and spine, which is really healing and helpful. I still leave some around the legs to enhance the flow of energy and put more at the top of the head.

Once the stones are placed, I put my hands in prayer position and say (typically to myself) "You are free to accept or reject this healing. May Higher Will be done."

As a healer, all you can do is send the energy, and then you must get out of the way. It's the same when you do your own self healing which is why, after all these years of teaching, I recommend you allow yourself to nap, because while you are resting, you are staying out of your own way. You are not worried about whether or not you can feel what's happening, and you are not over analyzing.

That's harder to do when you're working on someone else, because we all want others to get an amazing result. Just know the person will receive whatever is meant to be. That's it. That's all you can do!

By asking that Higher Will be done, you are letting the Universe know you want what is best for that person and you cannot know what's best for anyone but yourself, and even then, knowing the self is a challenging lifelong pursuit. So allow the healing to happen and stay out of the way.

Speaking of allowing…at the end of the session, bring your hands to prayer position and say, "Allow this healing to continue. May higher will be done."

In between the beginning and the end, I suggest taking a stone or Crystal in your hand and waving it over the person, imagining the Crystal is stimulating the subtle energy fields around the body, relieving the person of any stresses or worries. Imagine they are relaxed and feeling great, and that the session is of benefit to them in body, mind and spirit.

Send the other person love, happiness, hope, anything you feel they need, while imagining the Crystal clearing out the old and making way for the new, relieving them of worldly concerns and stresses, and making their lives happier, healthier and more abundant. It all starts with intention, so make sure your goal reflects the very best possible outcome for all concerned.

Group Healing

Have you ever participated in a group healing in Reiki or any other modality? It's an interesting experience. The receiver lies on a massage table, and everybody begins with a prayer, and starts sending the energy together.

When you use Crystals for group healing, you do the same thing, only you place the stones on the person before you begin sending the energy. You may find they need extra Crystals on a knee, for example, and you should always follow your instincts.

Once the stones or Crystals are in place, send energy with your hands, or use a Crystal in the hand to stir up the energy fields.

With the group, this may go on for ten minutes or so, and then something strangely interesting happens. Everyone gets a collective vibe that the healing is over, and normally everybody steps back at the same time, bringing their hands together in prayer.

Then, you collectively wish for the highest and best for the recipient, and then, the healing is complete.

And that's it! Easy, right?

Actually it is easy. Just know that you are a powerful being and trust your instincts. The Universal Manager will do the rest.

10
CONCLUSION

I hope you've enjoyed our Crystal journey and that this book has provided some new ideas or at least reminded you of things perhaps you haven't tried in awhile. At the very least, I hope this information will be of assistance to you in finding the right stones to work with and understanding what you've found once you align yourself with the special Crystals that you are meant to work with in this lifetime.

Crystals are our helpers and friends. Will we allow Crystals to support us so we can receive the gifts Mother Nature offers?

We are on an accelerated path in these interesting times. Crystals support us in fulfilling our mission on Earth and understanding the universe at large at a deeper level.

All we need is to allow them to show how they can best work with and for us, by encouraging us to experiment with new ways of healing for ourselves and others.

We are at a critical time. Everybody is needed to step up

their game in compassion and universal understanding to help our fellow man.

Crystals and the spirits who inhabit them are here for a reason, just like we are, to be present in this moment, and to participate in the cosmic experiment of life.

I hope we will ascend to the next phase of our collective development with grace and in respect for the dignity and importance of all sentient beings, and recognize the truth that all people are one.

Crystals open us up to the new energies coming in at this time. Won't you work with them and allow them to illuminate your path?

As always, I hope you enjoy the journey. Know I am wishing you great joy and peace in your life.

Namaste!

BIBLIOGRAPHIC NOTES

A few years ago if you would have told me Wikipedia would become such a reliable source of information, I would not have believed it, and yet, thanks to conscious contributors who do painstaking research, here we are. For your reference I've included a few links where you can explore more about the fascinating topic of Crystals. Enjoy!

Applied Kinesiology aka Muscle Testing:
https://en.wikipedia.org/wiki/Applied_kinesiology

Artemisia Tridentata aka Sage:
https://en.wikipedia.org/wiki/Artemisia_tridentata

Crystal Structure: https://en.wikipedia.org/wiki/Crystal_structure

Magnesium Sulfate aka Epsom Salt:
https://en.wikipedia.org/wiki/Magnesium_sulfate

Marcel Vogel: https://en.wikipedia.org/wiki/Marcel_Vogel

Mount Ida, Arkansas:
https://en.wikipedia.org/wiki/Mount_Ida,_Arkansas

Pendulum: https://en.wikipedia.org/wiki/Pendulum

Platonic Solids: https://en.wikipedia.org/wiki/Platonic_solid

Rutile: http://www.minerals.net/mineral/rutile.aspx

Sea Salt: https://en.wikipedia.org/wiki/Sea_salt

Have a question?
Send Dr. Shelley an email: shelley@shelleykaehr.com or visit her **Facebook Fan Page at Past Life Lady**

Printed in Great Britain
by Amazon

60557308R00037